Viola

SCALES FOR STRINGS

by SAMUEL APPLEBAUM

To be used
as supplementary studies to any string class method
or
as material to develop a string ensemble.

FOREWORD

The Belwin SCALES FOR STRINGS is to be used as supplementary material for any of the string class methods or as interesting training material for the development of a string orchestra.

Authorities agree that scales are indispensable for the development of intonation and a sound left-hand technic. In this Scale Book, the scales and arpeggios are presented in various rhythms and bowings.

In Book I, the basic, solid bowings are used, the détaché and martelé with the entire bow, as well as in different parts of the bow.

In each key there are melodies and rounds to be played in unison and with the class as a string ensemble. The melodies that represent each key are chosen because of their technical value and because they help to develop a sense of tonality in that particular key.

Book I includes the major keys of C, G, D, A, F, B♭ and E♭, in the first position.

THE SIGNS USED IN THIS BOOK

⊓ means down-bow. V means up-bow.
A note with a dot above or below means that the martelé bowing is to be used.
A.M. means to play above the middle of the bow.
B.M. means to play below the middle of the bow.
W.B. means whole bow (this term is approximate).
// means the bow is to be lifted. A comma (❜) means to leave a slight pause, with the bow remaining
   on the string - usually at the end of a phrase.
p means soft. *mp* means moderately soft. *pp* means very soft.
f means loud. *mf* means moderately loud. *ff* means very loud.
cresc. or ◁ means gradually louder.
dim. or ▷ means gradually softer.
rit. means gradually slower.
simile means that you are to continue in the same style of bowing.
∧ This sign indicates that there is a half-step between the two notes.
The letter P after a number indicates that there is a piano part for that melody.

THE KEY OF C MAJOR

What Is a Scale?

The word scale means a "ladder". A scale is a "ladder" of 8 notes in alphabetical order. If we play 8 notes, going up a step at a time, so that the 8th note is an octave above the 1st note, we have a scale.

What Is a Major Scale?

If there is a half step between the 3rd and 4th notes, and a half step between the 7th and 8th notes, we have a major scale. Between the other notes, there must be whole steps. If we start on C and build a major scale we call it a C major scale.

The C Major Scale

Notice the half steps between the 3rd and 4th notes and the 7th and 8th notes. When this sign ∧ connects two notes, it means that they are a half step apart.

Use the whole bow (W.B.) for each note.

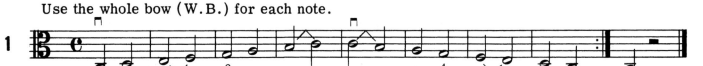

Here we have the C major scale starting on C an octave higher.
W.B. - Divide the bow evenly using a half bow for each note.

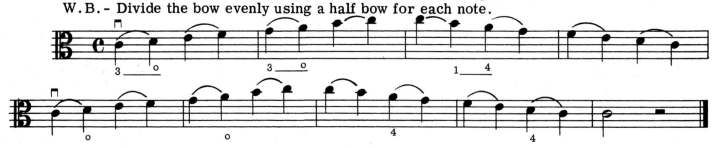

The Détaché Bowing

The Détaché is a smooth bowing that may be played in any part of the bow.
Practice this in 3 ways:
①*Above the middle (A.M.)* ②*Below the middle (B.M.)* ③*Pizzicato*

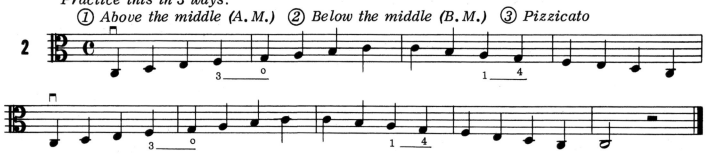

The Détaché Bowing Above and Below the Middle

A Melody In The Key Of C Major

A melody in the Key of C Major uses the notes that are in the C Major Scale. The letter P indicates that there is a piano part for that melody.

Saint Paul's Steeple

Broadly - in moderate time

ENGLISH FOLK SONG

The Martelé Bowing

The Martelé bowing starts with an accent followed by an immediate release. There is to be a clean stop between each note. This bowing may also be played in any part of the bow.

Practice in 3 ways:
① *The whole bow (W.B.)* ② *Above the middle (A.M.)* ③ *Below the middle (B.M.)*

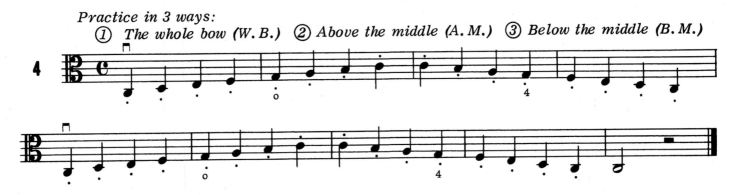

The Martelé Bowing Above and Below the Middle

The Détaché Bowing In 8th Notes

Practice in 2 ways: ① *A.M.* ② *B.M.*

E.L.1853

A Round In C Major

Good Night

Gracefully - in moderate time

The C Major Scale In Different Rhythms

(Memorize)

W.B. - Draw the bow quickly on the up-bow.

W.B. - Draw the bow quickly on the down-bow.

Our Class Becomes A String Ensemble

Spring Is Here

The small notes in the 1st and 9th measures are to be stopped by the finger but not played. **With spirit - in moderate time (Key of C)**   17th CENTURY MELODY

These Are Called Arpeggios Or Broken Chords

Use the Détaché bowing - *Practice in 3 ways:* ① W.B. ② A.M. ③ B.M.

Use the Martelé bowing - *Practice in 3 ways:* ① W.B. ② A.M. ③ B.M.

Arpeggios In Different Rhythms

W.B. - Draw the bow quickly on the up-bow.

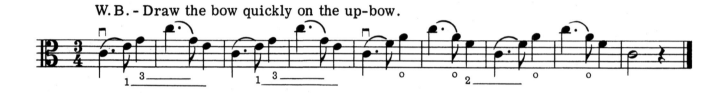

W.B. - Draw the bow quickly on the down-bow.

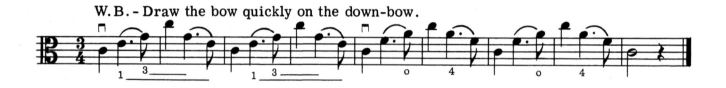

A Song To Thee

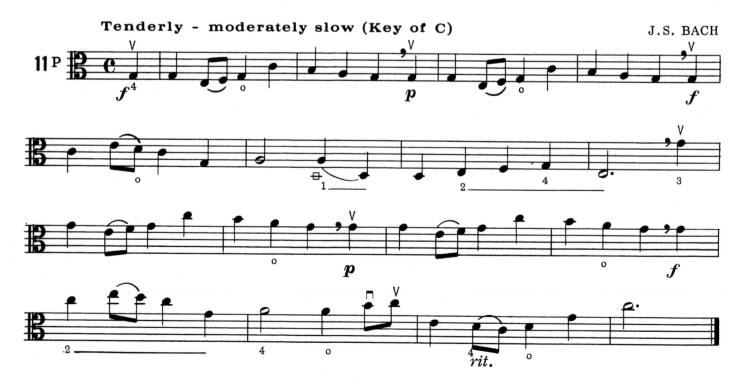

THE KEY OF G MAJOR

Here is a major scale that starts on the note G. Notice that a sharp has been placed before F. We know that in every major scale there must be a half step between the 3rd and 4th notes and the 7th and 8th notes. When we build a major scale that starts on G, we always raise the note F so that there will be a half step between the 7th and 8th notes.

The G Major Scale

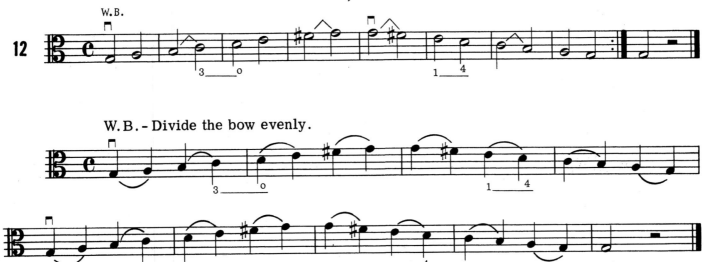

W.B. - Divide the bow evenly.

If we place a sharp in the signature on the space F, it will mean that every F throughout the scale is to be raised. The F sharps will be played with the 3rd finger on C and the 2nd finger on D.

The Détaché Bowing

Practice in 3 ways: ① *A.M.* ② *B.M.* ③ *Pizzicato*

The Détaché Bowing Above and Below the Middle

A Melody In The Key Of G Major

Auld Lang Syne

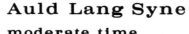

The Martelé Bowing In G Major

Practice in 3 ways: ① W.B. ② A.M. ③ B.M.

The Martelé Bowing Above and Below the Middle

The Détaché Bowing In 8th Notes

Practice in 2 ways: ① A.M. ② B.M.

A Round In G Major

Scotland's Burning

The G Major Scale In Different Rhythms
(Memorize)

18

W.B. - Draw the bow quickly on the up-bow.

W.B. - Draw the bow quickly on the down-bow.

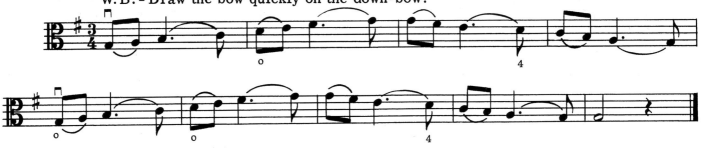

Arpeggios In G Major

Use the Détaché bowing - *Practice in 3 ways:* ① *W.B.* ② *A.M.* ③ *B.M.*

19

Use the Martelé bowing - *Practice in 3 ways:* ① *W.B.* ② *A.M.* ③ *B.M.*

Arpeggios In Different Rhythms

20

W.B. - Draw the bow quickly on the up-bow.

W.B. - Draw the bow quickly on the down-bow.

Ode To Joy
(String Ensemble)
Majestically - in moderate time (Key of G)

L. VAN BEETHOVEN

MELODY

21 P

ENSEMBLE

THE KEY OF D MAJOR

Here is a major scale that starts on the note D. Notice that sharps have been placed before F and C. We raise these notes so that there will be a half step between the 3rd and 4th notes and the 7th and 8th notes. When we build a major scale that starts on D, we always raise the notes F and C.

The D Major Scale

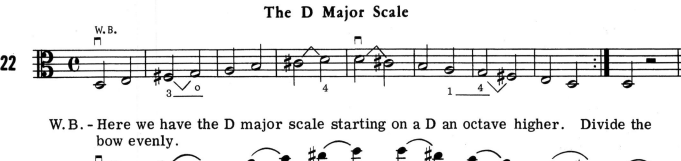

W.B. - Here we have the D major scale starting on a D an octave higher. Divide the bow evenly.

If we place the two sharps in the signature, it will mean that every F and C throughout the scale is to be raised. The F sharps will be played with the 3rd on C and the 2nd on D. The C sharps will be played with the 3rd on G and the 2nd on A.

The Détaché Bowing

Practice in 3 ways: ① *A.M.* ② *B.M.* ③ *Pizzicato*

The Détaché Bowing Above and Below the Middle

A Melody In The Key Of D Major
Our Graduation Song

With spirit - in moderate time

WILLIAM BRADBURY

Refrain

The Martelé Bowing In D Major

Practice in 3 ways: ① W.B. ② A.M. ③ B.M.

The Martelé Bowing Above and Below the Middle

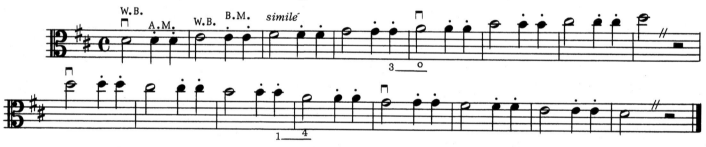

The Détaché Bowing In 8th Notes

Practice in 2 ways: ① A.M. ② B.M.

A Round In D Major
Are You Sleeping?

Brightly - moderately fast

ONE   TWO   THREE   ROUND IN FOUR PARTS
                                         FOUR

The D Major Scale In Different Rhythms
(Memorize)

28

W.B. - Draw the bow quickly on the up-bow.

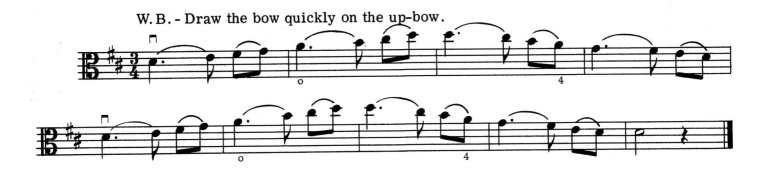

W.B. - Draw the bow quickly on the down-bow.

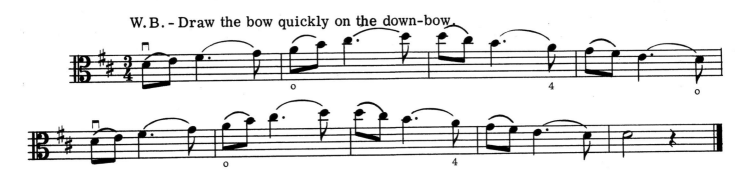

Arpeggios In D Major

Use the Détaché bowing - *Practice in 3 ways:* ① *W.B.* ② *A.M.* ③ *B.M.*

29

Use the Martelé bowing - *Practice in 3 ways:* ① *W.B.* ② *A.M.* ③ *B.M.*

Arpeggios In Different Rhythms

W.B. - Draw the bow quickly on the up-bow.

W.B. - Draw the bow quickly on the down-bow.

Deck The Hall

(String Ensemble)
With spirit - moderately fast (Key of D)

OLD WELSH AIR

THE KEY OF A MAJOR

Here is a major scale that starts on the note A. Notice that sharps have been placed before F, C and G. We raise these notes so that there will be a half step between the 3rd and 4th notes and the 7th and 8th notes. When we build a major scale that starts on A, we always raise the notes F, C and G.

The A Major Scale

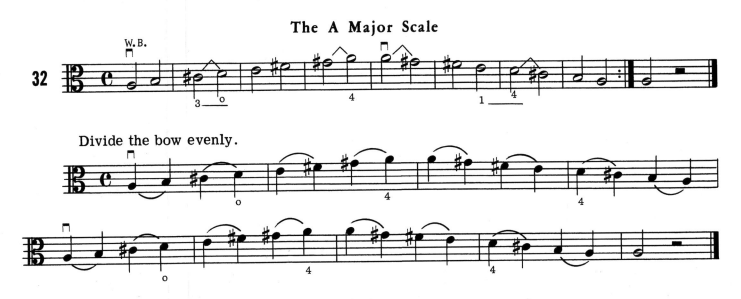

If we place the three sharps in the signature, it will mean that every F, C and G throughout the scale is to be raised. The F sharps will be played with the 3rd on C and the 2nd on D. The C sharps will be played with the 3rd on G and the 2nd on A. The open C string is sharped by placing the first finger close to the nut. The G sharps will be played with the 3rd on D. The open G string is sharped by placing the 1st finger close to the nut.

The Détaché Bowing

Practice in 3 ways: ① A.M. ② B.M. ③ Pizzicato

The Détaché Bowing Above and Below the Middle

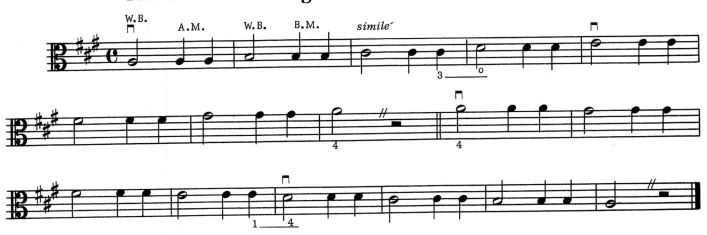

E.L.1853

A Melody In The Key Of A Major

Red River Valley

With feeling - moderately slow

COWBOY SONG

The Martelé Bowing In A Major

Practice in 3 ways: ① *W. B.* ② *A. M.* ③ *B. M.*

The Martelé Bowing Above and Below the Middle

The Détaché Bowing In 8th Notes

Practice in 2 ways: ① *A. M.* ② *B. M.*

A Round In A Major

Early To Bed

Gracefully - in moderate time

ROUND IN THREE PARTS

The A Major Scale In Different Rhythms
(Memorize)

W.B. - Draw the bow quickly on the up-bow.

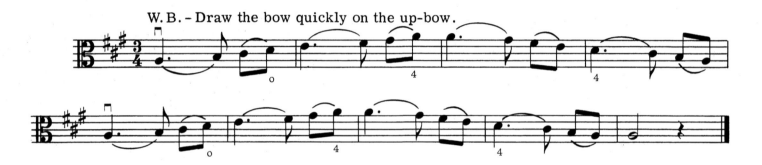

W.B. - Draw the bow quickly on the down-bow.

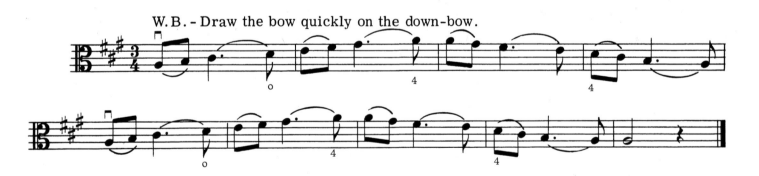

Arpeggios In A Major

Use the Détaché bowing - *Practice in 3 ways:* ① *W.B.* ② *A.M.* ③ *B.M.*

Use the Martelé bowing - *Practice in 3 ways:* ① *W.B.* ② *A.M.* ③ *B.M.*

Arpeggios In Different Rhythms

W.B. – Draw the bow quickly on the up-bow.

W.B. – Draw the bow quickly on the down-bow.

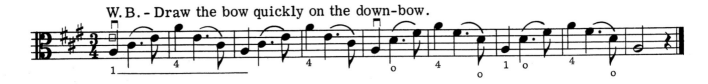

Adeste Fideles
(String Ensemble)

Joyfully – in moderate time (Key of A)

J. READING

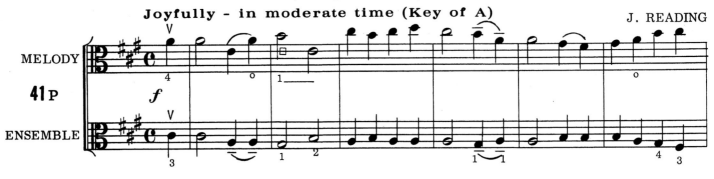

Refrain

THE KEY OF F MAJOR

Here is a major scale that starts on the note F. Notice that a flat has been placed before B. We lower this note so that there will be a half step between the 3rd and 4th notes. When we build a major scale that starts on F we always lower the note B.

The F Major Scale

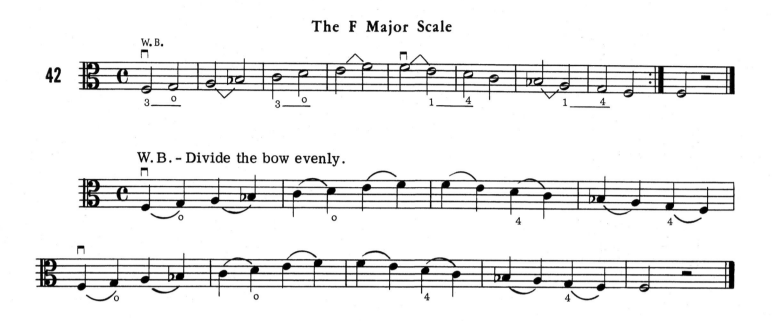

If we place the flat in the signature on the space B, it will mean that every B throughout the scale is to be lowered. The B flats will be played with the 2nd on G, and the 1st on A.

The Détaché Bowing

Practice in 3 ways: ① *A.M.* ② *B.M.* ③ *Pizzicato*

The Détaché Bowing Above and Below the Middle

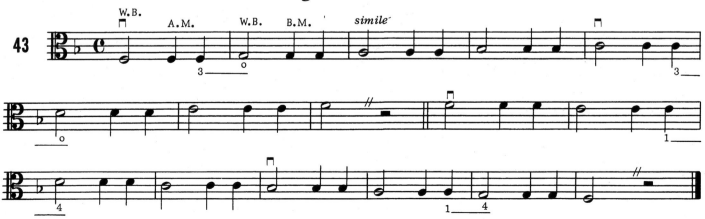

A Melody In F Major
La Ra La

Gaily - moderately fast

W.A. MOZART

The Martelé Bowing In F Major

Practice in 3 ways: ① W.B. ② A.M. ③ B.M.

The Martelé Bowing Above and Below the Middle

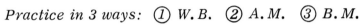

The Détaché Bowing In 8th Notes

Practice in 2 ways: ① A.M. ② B.M.

A Round In F Major
Lovely Evening

Gracefully - moderately fast

ROUND IN THREE PARTS

The F Major Scale In Different Rhythms

(Memorize)

W. B. - Draw the bow quickly on the up-bow.

W. B. - Draw the bow quickly on the down-bow.

Arpeggios In F Major

Use the Détaché bowing - *Practice in 3 ways:* ① *W. B.* ② *A. M.* ③ *B. M.*

Use the Martelé bowing - *Practice in 3 ways:* ① *W. B.* ② *A. M.* ③ *B. M.*

Arpeggios In Different Rhythms

50

W.B. - Draw the bow quickly on the up-bow.

W.B. - Draw the bow quickly on the down-bow.

See, The Conquering Hero Comes

(String Ensemble)

With dignity - in moderate time (Key of F)

G.F. HANDEL

MELODY

51P

ENSEMBLE

D.C. al Fine

THE KEY OF B FLAT MAJOR

Here is a major scale that starts on the note B flat. Notice that flats have been placed before B and E. We lower these notes so that there will be a half step between the 3rd and 4th notes, and the 7th and 8th notes. When we build a major scale that starts on B flat, we always lower the notes B and E.

The B♭ Major Scale

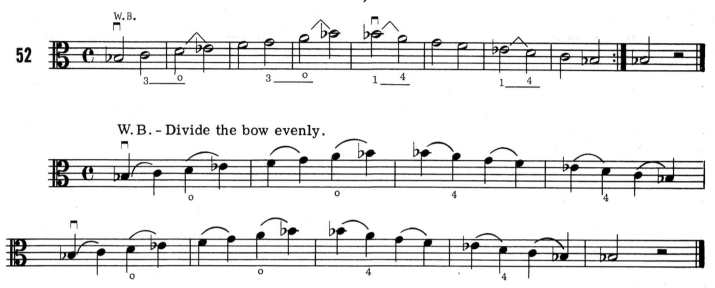

52

W.B. - Divide the bow evenly.

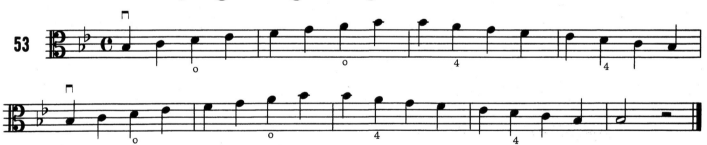

If we place the two flats in the signature it will mean that every B and E throughout the scale is to be lowered. The B flats will be played with the 2nd on G and the 1st on A. The E flats will be played with the 2nd on C, 1st on D, and 4th on A.

The Détaché Bowing

Practice in 3 ways: ① *A.M.* ② *B.M.* ③ *Pizzicato*

53

The Détaché Bowing Above and Below the Middle

A Melody In The Key Of B♭ Major

The Old Oaken Bucket

E. KAILLMARK

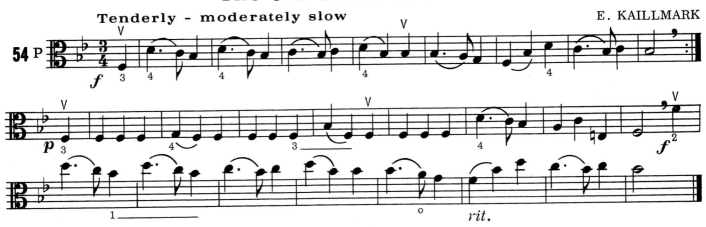

The Martelé Bowing In B♭ Major

Practice in 3 ways: ① W.B. ② A.M. ③ B.M.

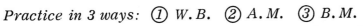

The Martelé Bowing Above and Below the Middle

The Détaché Bowing In 8th Notes

Practice in 2 ways: ① A.M. ② B.M.

A Round In B♭ Major

Ice Skating

ROUND IN THREE PARTS

The B♭ Major Scale In Different Rhythms

(Memorize)

W.B. - Draw the bow quickly on the up-bow.

W.B. - Draw the bow quickly on the down-bow.

Arpeggios In B♭ Major

Use the Détaché bowing - *Practice in 3 ways:* ① W.B. ② A.M. ③ B.M.

Use the Martelé bowing - *Practice in 3 ways:* ① W.B. ② A.M. ③ B.M.

E.L.1853

Arpeggios In Different Rhythms

60

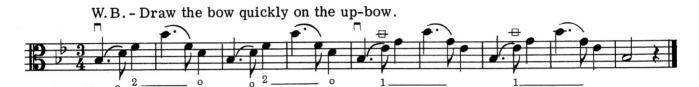

W.B. - Draw the bow quickly on the up-bow.

W.B. - Draw the bow quickly on the down-bow.

Marching On!

(String Ensemble)

Majestically - in moderate time (Key of B♭)

JOHN GOSS

MELODY

61 P

ENSEMBLE

THE KEY OF E FLAT MAJOR

Here is a major scale that starts on the note E flat. Notice that flats have been placed before B, E and A. We lower these notes so that there will be a half step between the 3rd and 4th and the 7th and 8th notes. When we build a major scale that starts on E flat, we always lower the notes B, E and A.

The E♭ Major Scale

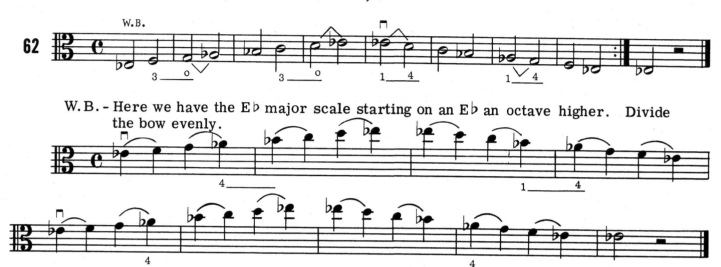

W.B. - Here we have the E♭ major scale starting on an E♭ an octave higher. Divide the bow evenly.

If we place the three flats in the signature it will mean that every B, E and A throughout the scale is to be lowered. The B flats will be played with the 2nd on G and the 1st on A. The E flats will be played with the 2nd on C, the 1st on D and the 4th on A. The A flats will be played with the 1st on G and the 4th on D.

The Détaché Bowing

Practice in 3 ways: ① *A.M.* ② *B.M.* ③ *Pizzicato*

The Détaché Bowing Above and Below the Middle

A Melody In The Key Of Eb Major

The Green Hill

TRADITIONAL WELSH MELODY

The Martelé Bowing In Eb Major

Practice in 3 ways: ① W.B. ② A.M. ③ B.M.

The Martelé Bowing Above and Below the Middle

The Détaché Bowing In 8th Notes

Practice in 2 ways: ① A.M. ② B.M.

A Round In Eb Major

For Fun

Joyfully- in moderate time

ROUND IN FOUR PARTS

The Eb Major Scale In Different Rhythms

(Memorize)

68

W.B. – Draw the bow quickly on the up-bow.

W.B. – Draw the bow quickly on the down-bow.

Arpeggios In Eb Major

Use the Détaché bowing - *Practice in 3 ways:* ① *W.B.* ② *A.M.* ③ *B.M.*

69

Use the Martelé bowing - *Practice in 3 ways:* ① *W.B.* ② *A.M.* ③ *B.M.*

E.L.1853

Arpeggios In Different Rhythms

W.B. - Draw the bow quickly on the up-bow.

W.B. - Draw the bow quickly on the down-bow.

Air

(String Ensemble)

Tenderly - moderately slow (Key of E♭)

F.J. HAYDN

MELODY

71 P

ENSEMBLE